T0021054

INVENTOR, ENGINEER, AND PHYSICIST

NIKOLA TESLA

KATIE MARSICO

Lerner Publications ◆ Minneapolis

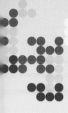

To my husband, Carl—another extremely talented engineer

Lerner Publications Company
A division of Lerner Publishing Group, Inc.
241 First Avenue North
Minneapolis, MN 55401 USA

For reading levels and more information, look up this title at www.lernerbooks.com.

Content consultant: W. Bernard Carlson, Professor and Chair, Engineering & Society Department, University of Virginia

Library of Congress Cataloging-in-Publication Data

Names: Marsico, Katie, 1980–
Title: Inventor, engineer, and physicist Nikola Tesla / by Katie Marsico.
Description: Minneapolis : Lerner Publications, [2018] | Series: STEM trailblazer bios | Audience: Age 7–11. | Audience: Grade 4 to 6. | Includes bibliographical references and index.
Identifiers: LCCN 2016049276 (print) | LCCN 2016050368 (ebook) | ISBN 9781512434484 (lb : alk. paper) | ISBN 9781512456301 (pb : alk. paper) | ISBN 9781512451009 (eb pdf)
Subjects: LCSH: Tesla, Nikola, 1856–1943—Juvenile literature. | Electrical engineers—United States—Biography—Juvenile literature. | Inventors—United States—Biography—Juvenile literature.
Classification: LCC TK140.T4 M1957 2018 (print) | LCC TK140.T4 (ebook) | DDC 621.3092 [B] — dc23

LC record available at https://lccn.loc.gov/2016049276

Manufactured in the United States of America
1-42097-25391-2/22/2017

The images in this book are used with the permission of: © Bettmann/Getty Images, p. 4; William James Bennett after John Robert Murray, Niagara Falls from the American Side, Collection of Mr. and Mrs. Paul Mellon, Image courtesy of the Board of Trustees, National Gallery of Art, Washington DC, p. 6; © Internet Archive Book Images/flickr.com, p. 8; Wikimedia Commons, pp. 9, 15, 28; © Science and Society/SuperStock, p. 10; © Stefano Bianchetti/Corbis Historical/Getty Images, p. 13; Photoshot/Newscom, p. 14; © Everett Historical/Shutterstock.com, p. 16; AP Photo, p. 18; Chronicle/Alamy Stock Photo, p. 20; Everett Collection Inc/Alamy Stock Photo, p. 23; Bygone Collection/Alamy Stock Photo, p. 24; © Chicago History Museum/Archive Photos/Getty Images, p. 25; Wikimedia Commons (CC BY 4.0), p. 26.

Front cover: Library of Congress (LC-B2- 1026-9).

Main body text set in Adrianna Regular 13/22. Typeface provided by Chank.

CONTENTS

Chapter 1

Tesla's interest in inventing began early, when he was a boy in Croatia.

IMAGINING
POSSIBILITIES

On July 10, 1856, Nikola Tesla was born in Smiljan, Lika (modern-day Croatia). A bad thunderstorm rumbled overhead just as Nikola arrived. To some people, the dark clouds seemed like an unlucky sign. Would Nikola's life be cursed?

Nikola's mother said no. As lightning flashed across the night sky, she predicted he would have a bright future. Years later, Nikola proved her right. He became a famous inventor, **engineer**, and **physicist**. His most famous inventions involved electricity.

Nikola's childhood was shaped by science and creative thinking. His mother was a skilled inventor who designed several unique home appliances, including a mechanical eggbeater. Watching her sparked Nikola's curiosity about the way things work.

Nikola's father was a priest in the Serbian Orthodox Church. He hoped Nikola would follow in his footsteps. But Nikola was far more interested in science than religion.

Even as a boy, Nikola thought like an engineer. He was fascinated by natural forces and imagined incredible possibilities that didn't occur to most children. Nikola was deeply inspired by a steel engraving, or carving, of Niagara Falls in New York. When he studied the image, he saw more than rushing water. In his vision, the falls were turning a giant wheel. Nikola believed this wheel could be used to harness the energy of the falls.

It would be a while before Nikola conquered Niagara Falls. Meanwhile, he built unique machines on the family farm. Not all of them worked. Nikola designed a glider—an aircraft without an engine—from an umbrella. Unfortunately, the invention failed to make him fly. When Nikola leapt off the roof of his house, the glider simply crashed to the ground with him. His injuries kept him in bed for six weeks, but they didn't slow the flow of Nikola's creative ideas.

When young Nikola saw a picture of Niagara Falls, he imagined a wheel that could turn the waterfall's power into usable energy.

As a student, Nikola impressed his teachers with his quick mind and sharp memory. He easily performed complicated math problems in his head. In fact, Nikola was so skilled that teachers sometimes suspected him of cheating!

EXPLORING ELECTROMAGNETISM

In 1873, Nikola became seriously ill. He had cholera, a dangerous infection that causes severe stomach problems. For months, he struggled to recover. His father promised that Nikola could attend engineering school if he got better. By 1875, the young man had regained his health and was attending college in Austria.

One day during class, Nikola's physics teacher demonstrated the transmission of electricity using a motor and a generator called a dynamo. When a student turned a crank, the dynamo used **electromagnetism** to make an electric **current**. The current flowed through a wire to the motor on the other side of the room. Then the motor used the electricity to produce motion.

During the nineteenth century, electricity was a new and exciting power source. As Nikola watched this mysterious motor spark and hum, he believed he could make it better.

Chapter 2

In the nineteenth century, before modern electricity, most machinery was powered by steam. This steam pipe system and generator provided energy for subway trains in the 1880s.

EARLY ENGINEERING
EFFORTS

Seeing the electric dynamo and motor in action increased Tesla's interest in electricity. Before his teacher's presentation had ended, he was already thinking of design improvements. Tesla suggested getting rid of moving parts called commutators.

Tesla's teacher made fun of him for describing the impossible. After all, commutators helped the electrical current get into both the dynamo and the motor.

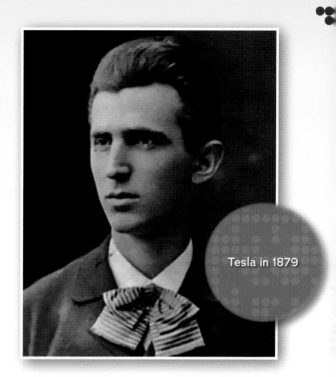

Tesla in 1879

Early electric motors were powered by direct-current (DC) electricity. They used two pairs of **electromagnets**. The current flowed in one direction through a coil, or series of wire loops, called a rotor. The rotor was the first pair of electromagnets. It was free to move. The second set of electromagnets—the stator—was fixed. When the similar poles of the two magnetic fields repelled each other, the rotor spun.

Most electric motors at the time relied on commutators to reverse the direction of the current. That caused the rotor's magnetic field to push away from the stators in the motor's frame. Without the commutators and constant current, the rotor stopped spinning. If the rotor didn't spin, the motor didn't work.

Commutators weren't perfect. They were expensive. They also sparked. That meant the machine produced less power. Tesla's answer was a motor that didn't rely on commutators to control the current's flow. He suspected the solution was currents that alternated, or changed, direction. During the 1870s, most scientists didn't understand how alternating current (AC) could be more practical than DC power. Tesla believed he'd eventually be able to show them. First, though, he had to figure out how to build a motor that ran on AC power.

Tesla's sketch for an AC motor led to the polyphase induction motor. The first working model was finished in 1888.

DESIGNING A BETTER MOTOR

At school, Tesla focused on electrical engineering. But he lost his scholarship in his third year and had to leave college.

In 1881, Tesla moved to Budapest, Hungary, to work at the Central Telegraph Office. His job was to improve early equipment that could send messages long distances. The job didn't pay much, and Tesla soon quit so he could focus on developing a better motor.

Tesla made difficult choices for the sake of his research. He was so focused on designing a better motor that he often stayed awake all night. As days passed without a breakthrough, he grew tired and frustrated. Tesla never gave up, though, and his efforts paid off.

FINALLY FIGURING OUT THE ANSWER

One evening in 1882, Tesla strolled through a city park with a friend. As he walked, a vision came to him. It was a solution to the problem Tesla had been working so hard to solve. Suddenly he knew how to build a motor using AC power! Tesla hadn't brought a pen and paper to the park. So he sketched his design in the sand with a stick.

In all electric motors, the two sets of electromagnets push away from each other. This repelling force makes the shaft on the motor turn. Before Tesla, engineers used a commutator to change the direction of the current flowing through the rotor. That caused the magnets to repel each other.

Tesla's insight was to get rid of the commutator. He used AC to change the magnetic field in the stator. Another advantage over earlier models was that Tesla could create more than one wave of electricity, providing more power. Tesla's invention—the polyphase induction motor—would forever change the face of electricity.

Tesla with his magnifying transmitter, which could transfer electrical currents as strong as lightning

Chapter 3

Tesla in his lab in the late nineteenth century

OPPORTUNITIES IN
OTHER COUNTRIES

Tesla soon began a job at the Continental Edison Company in Paris, France. The job seemed perfect for him. Tesla was asked to make design improvements on electrical equipment. Another benefit was that US inventor Thomas Edison owned the company from overseas.

Edison was already world famous. He had invented everything from the **phonograph** to the first practical electric lightbulb. Edison was also trying to find better ways of distributing electrical power.

Edison founded several companies to work on different projects. Edison Machine Works in New York City focused on making dynamos.

EDISON MACHINE WORKS.

OFFICE

TRYING TO ATTRACT INVESTORS

Tesla hoped that the company would be interested in his AC motor. He had finally built a working model that he demonstrated in June 1883. Yet Tesla didn't have the money to take his invention to the next level. To develop the motor for widespread use, he needed the support of **investors**.

The first power plant in the United States opened in 1882. It was able to light four hundred lamps at one time.

TECH TALK

"One of the great events in my life was my first meeting with Edison. This wonderful man, who had received no scientific training, yet had accomplished so much, filled me with amazement."

—*Nikola Tesla*

Several people were fascinated by Tesla's efforts. But most were still convinced that DC electricity was a better power source. Finally, a manager at the company suggested heading to the United States, where investors might be more open to new technology. Since the manager knew Edison, he wrote him a letter of introduction on Tesla's behalf.

INVENTORS WITH DIFFERENT OPINIONS

In the summer of 1884, Tesla set sail for New York City. Once there, he began a job with Edison Machine Works. It wasn't long before Tesla's work attracted Edison's attention. The older inventor was impressed by his new employee's engineering skills.

Many of the electrical wires in New York City were knocked down by a blizzard in 1888.

Tesla repaired and improved Edison's dynamos, among other things. Edison was pleased. Yet he refused to consider Tesla's motor—or AC power in general. Much of Edison's fame and wealth were rooted in DC electricity.

Edison's DC power lines stretched across a growing number of communities. His electrical system shed light on city streets and inside people's homes. Edison respected Tesla. But he wasn't about to be overshadowed by AC technology. Instead, he urged Tesla to focus on further developing DC power. At one point, Edison supposedly offered him $50,000 to improve the design of a DC lighting system.

Tesla jumped at the challenge. He even designed a new system for Edison. Yet Tesla never received payment. Edison claimed he had only been joking about the $50,000. In 1885, Tesla quit working for him.

Chapter 4

This illustration shows Tesla holding electric lamps powered wirelessly by the machine behind him.

WINNING A
SCIENTIFIC WAR

At first, Tesla struggled after leaving Edison Machine Works. Desperate for a job, he dug ditches for two dollars a day. Eventually, however, Tesla's luck began to change. He became friends with Alfred Brown, the man overseeing his work.

Brown and attorney Charles Peck were interested in Tesla's ideas about AC power. In exchange for a percentage of any money earned from Tesla's inventions, they agreed to become his investors.

In 1887, the Tesla Electric Light and Manufacturing Company started operating out of a laboratory in New York City. Money from investors let Tesla focus on perfecting his motor. He soon filed for a patent on it. This government-issued license gives only the owner of a patent the right to produce or sell a particular invention.

Tesla also applied for patents on several other inventions that year. These inventions featured into his design for an entire electrical system based on AC power. This system would spark a famous competition that pitted Tesla against Edison. Their scientific battle would later become known as the War of the Currents.

TECH TALK

"That is the trouble with many inventors; they lack patience. They lack the willingness to work a thing out slowly and clearly and sharply in their mind, so that they can actually 'feel it work.' . . . We all make mistakes, and it is better to make them before we begin."

—Nikola Tesla

ADVANTAGES OF AC

In 1882, Edison had opened a power station in New York City. Inside, a steam engine turned the shafts of multiple dynamos. This created DC electricity. When the electricity left the plant, it traveled across power lines.

Yet the farther the current had to flow, the weaker it became. To travel longer distances, an electric current needs higher voltage, or force. A current with low voltage can't travel as far as one with higher voltage.

Sometimes the voltage had to be lowered, for safe distribution within homes and businesses. It was difficult to change the voltage of DC currents. Edison worked around these challenges by building a power station every few miles.

To Tesla, Edison's expensive DC system didn't make sense. The way DC currents traveled wasted power. Tesla also knew that it was easier to raise or lower the voltage of AC electricity. Tesla's system featured several phases of currents, which alternated direction many times per second. They also passed through transformers, machines that increased or decreased voltage as needed. Tesla could distribute currents long distances without losing much electricity.

George Westinghouse and Tesla used Tesla's AC technology to make this generator, completed in 1898.

WORKING WITH WESTINGHOUSE

In May 1888, Tesla presented his ideas about AC electricity to the American Institute of Electrical Engineers. Some members of the audience worked for the Westinghouse Electric and Manufacturing Company, owned by George Westinghouse. Edison and Westinghouse were rivals. Both men manufactured dynamos and sold electric lighting systems.

Westinghouse hoped an AC system would give him a competitive edge. After hearing reports of Tesla, he offered to purchase Tesla's patents. Tesla accepted the offer, and Westinghouse engineers began using his technology to power streetcars and factory machines.

Soon Westinghouse was selling a lot of AC equipment. Unsurprisingly, Edison viewed this as a threat. He responded by spreading rumors that AC was dangerous. According to Edison, AC power posed a much greater threat of electrocution than DC electricity. Yet there wasn't much proof to back up these statements.

In 1893, the World's Columbian Exposition was held in Chicago, Illinois. It was a massive fair celebrating the four hundredth anniversary of Christopher Columbus's arrival in North America. Westinghouse said he could electrify the event for $155,000 less than Edison. So the fair organizers hired him to supply power.

The administration building of the 1893 World's Columbian Exposition

Chicago's State Street during the 1893 World's Columbian Exposition

On May 1, US president Grover Cleveland kicked off opening night ceremonies with the flick of a switch. In a single moment, one hundred thousand electric lights glimmered over fairgoers' heads. To many people who had been following the War of the Currents, it was clear that Tesla and his AC system had won.

Chapter 5

Tesla tests electrical equipment in his lab in 1901.

POWERING THE
MODERN WORLD

After the fair, AC electricity quickly gained popularity. During the late nineteenth and early twentieth centuries, Tesla registered more than one hundred patents! He explored everything from fluorescent lighting and laser beams to remote-control devices and robotics. When he wasn't in his lab, he gave scientific speeches throughout the United States and Europe.

HARNESSING NIAGARA FALLS

In the 1890s, investors began planning a hydroelectric power plant at Niagara Falls in New York. Water from the falls would turn a **turbine**, which would then drive an electric generator. The investors hoped to transmit the resulting power first to the city of Buffalo and then to the rest of New York State. They decided to use Tesla's AC for distribution instead of Edison's DC.

Tesla was finally able to make his childhood dream of harnessing the power of the falls a reality. In 1895, the Niagara power plant opened. It featured Westinghouse AC generators based on Tesla's patents. This marked the first time Tesla's AC system could be used to produce electricity on a large scale.

TECH TALK

"What the result of these investigations will be the future will tell; but . . . I shall be [satisfied if] I have contributed a share, however small, to the advancement of science."

—*Nikola Tesla*

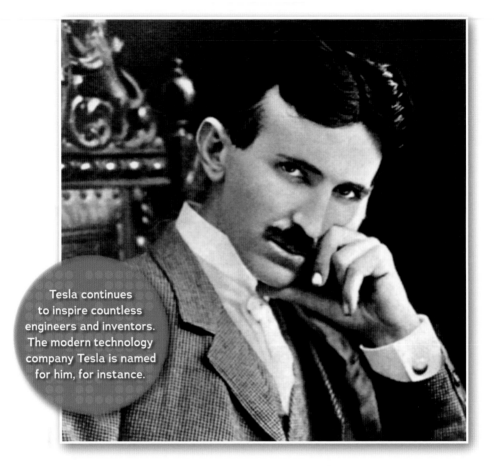

Tesla continues to inspire countless engineers and inventors. The modern technology company Tesla is named for him, for instance.

ACHIEVEMENTS THAT LIVE ON

Tesla, who died of a heart attack in New York City on January 7, 1943, had earned fame and respect across the globe. AC electricity continues to power much of the modern world. People use it for lighting, heating, cooling, transportation, and entertainment. This wouldn't be the case without Tesla, an inventor who didn't believe in the word *impossible*.

TIMELINE

1856
Nikola Tesla is born in Smiljan, Lika (Croatia), on July 10.

1881
Tesla moves to Budapest, Hungary, to work at the Central Telegraph Office.

1882
Tesla sketches his earliest design for a polyphase induction motor. Later that year, he moves to Paris to take a job with the Continental Edison Company.

1884
Tesla arrives in New York City to take a job with Edison Machine Works.

1885
Feeling cheated out of a $50,000 fee for a project, Tesla quits his job with Edison Machine Works.

1887
Tesla opens the Tesla Electric and Manufacturing Company in New York City. He soon applies for patents for the first practical motor using an AC system.

1888
Tesla presents his ideas about AC to the American Institute of Electrical Engineers. Word gets back to George Westinghouse, who will ultimately purchase several of Tesla's patents.

1893
Tesla's AC system is used to power electric lights at the World's Columbian Exposition. Many people consider this moment a sign of Tesla's victory in the War of the Currents.

1895
A hydroelectric power plant is completed at Niagara Falls in New York. It marks the first time Tesla's AC system is used on a large scale.

1943
Tesla dies in New York City on January 7, having registered more than one hundred patents during his lifetime.

SOURCE NOTES

5 Nikola Tesla, *My Inventions: Nikola Tesla's Autobiography* (Eastford, CT: Martino Fine Books, 2011), 14.

11 Ibid. 16–17.

17 M. K. Wisehart, "Making Your Imagination Work for You," *American Magazine*, April 1921, https://teslauniverse.com/nikola-tesla/articles/making-your-imagination-work-you.

21 George Heli Guy, "Tesla, Man and Inventor," *New York Times*, March 31, 1895, https://teslauniverse.com/nikola-tesla/articles/tesla-man-and-inventor.

27 Nikola Tesla, "Inventor Tesla Replies to Dr. Louis Duncan, Explaining His Alternating Current Motor," *Electrical Review*, June 2, 1888, https://teslauniverse.com/nikola-tesla/articles/inventor-tesla-replies-dr-louis-duncan-explaining-his-alternating-current.

GLOSSARY

current
an electrical flow

electromagnetism
the relationship between electricity and magnetism

electromagnets
devices made of a wire coil surrounding a soft metal center. Electromagnets become magnets when electrical current flows through the coil.

engineer
a specially trained person who designs or builds machines or systems

investors
people who help pay for a company's expenses and share in its profits

phonograph
an early sound-reproducing machine

physicist
a scientist who specializes in the study of matter and energy

turbine
a machine that creates power when the force of a liquid or gas is used to continuously turn a wheel

FURTHER INFORMATION

BOOKS

Marsico, Katie. *Electricity Investigations*. Minneapolis: Lerner Publications, 2018. Learn the backstory of the amazing force that fascinated Tesla.

Marsico, Katie. *Key Discoveries in Physical Science*. Minneapolis: Lerner Publications, 2015. Get an overview of the history of magnetism, electricity, and other physical forces.

Rusch, Elizabeth. *Electrical Wizard: How Nikola Tesla Lit Up the World*. Somerville, MA: Candlewick, 2013. Why was Tesla considered ahead of his time? Read more about this famous inventor and his impact on the modern world.

WEBSITES

Alliant Energy (AE) Kids: Energy Inventors
http://www.alliantenergykids.com/energybasics/energyinventors
Find out more about Tesla, as well as several other scientists responsible for major electrical breakthroughs.

Explain That Stuff! Electricity
http://www.explainthatstuff.com/electricity.html
Head here for further information on electrical currents, electromagnetism, and more!

Science Kids: Nikola Tesla Facts
http://www.sciencekids.co.nz/sciencefacts/scientists/nikolatesla.html
Check out this site for further information on Tesla's discoveries.

LERNER

SOURCE

Expand learning beyond the printed book. Download free, complementary educational resources for this book from our website, www.lernerresource.com.

INDEX

ABOUT THE AUTHOR

Katie Marsico has written more than two hundred nonfiction books for kids and young adults. Before becoming an author, she edited children's reference books. Marsico graduated from the Medill School of Journalism at Northwestern University. She lives in a suburb of Chicago with her husband and six children.